Postcolonial Literary Criticism
An Introductory Handbook

Yonge Eglinton

Copyright © 2019 Textual Matters
Cover: Ebrahim Khabazi
All rights reserved.
ISBN: 9781696219242

For Milad

CONTENTS

Introduction	1
Textual Analysis	3
Ideological Foundations of the Text	4
Colonization: Process and Dynamics	10
Language and Form	39
Readership and the Canon	44
Historical And Biographical Evidence	48
Positionality	49

1- Introduction

In the early twentieth century, with dwindling popularity of formalist approaches to literature such as New Criticism and Structuralism, postmodernist interest in ideological layers of literary texts created space for the emergence of activist literary approaches such as feminism and queer theory, but also postcolonial criticism. These approaches gained traction thanks to post-structuralist theories that made sense of literary works not only based on their internal formal elements but also by how they connected with the world and its people. These theories viewed text as an artifact in relation with social discourses, historical contexts, and power relations. As a case in point, postcolonial critics believed that an important component of literary analysis should be the study of how minoritized populations were portrayed in literature and also what kind of literature they produced and how their literary products were received.

It was not until scholars from colonized and racially minoritized populations found their way into mainstream Western academic establishments and started to write in European languages that postcolonial criticism would become appreciated in intellectual circles in Europe and North America. This appreciation—somehow a moral awakening among "white" European and American thinkers in a postcolonial world—was also the result of some historical factors. During the Cold War literary criticism in America and western

Europe was dominated by formalistic approaches, largely as an ideological reaction to Marxist literary theory's emphasis on the political and social contexts of literary works. After the collapse of the USSR, political readings of texts with an interest in class and race were deemed less dangerous and subversive in the capitalist West and thus started to be tolerated. Hence, literary analyses that centered around power and identity became an important component of the soul-searching performed by western colonizers and their offspring in a quieter post-war world. This was a pattern that would repeat in the wake of horrific historical experiences such as slavery in the United States, the Holocaust in Europe, and the suffering of aboriginal populations wherever they contacted European colonizers. As a result, along with other social justice oriented approaches to literature, postcolonial studies became an important discipline in humanities departments in western academia.

Postcolonial theory examines texts written by colonizers and the colonized in the course of colonization and also after that as a means of understanding the dynamics of colonialism. Postcolonial critics comb historical sources and collect data that can shed light on imperial dynamics. They study the literature written in European and native languages. They examine texts written by white colonizers and by postcolonial communities living in European or colonized lands. They read the literature written by slaves, immigrants, the displaced, minorities, racialized populations, and aboriginal writers. They unearth minority literatures omitted from the canon or ignored in mainstream literature. They revive native forms and genres. They also analyze the views and perceptions of readers of colonial and postcolonial literature.

It should be noted that postcolonial theory—similar to feminist theory, queer criticism, and ecocriticism—has an overt ideological and political edge and is thus meant to be transformative. Postcolonial critics are often transparent about their positionality, sociocultural agenda, and political views. Many confirm that their work, although academically rigorous, is a form of activism beyond an obsession with textual literariness and formal beauty. This tendency, however, does not mean that postcolonial literary theorists have not written about literary forms and are not concerned with aesthetics. On the contrary, by magnifying the sociopolitical layers of literature, postcolonial theorists show that aesthetics are not objective, disinterested, or neutral. They show Western literary and artistic canons have been politically constructed to put white Europeans' literature on the pedestal and disregard black, native, and aboriginal aesthetics. In this pamphlet we discuss all of these points of interest at an introductory level. We first focus on how postcolonial critics try to make sense of colonial dynamics through textual analysis. Next, we focus on language and form. Finally, we discuss why postcolonial theory is also interested in how readers have reacted to colonial (and postcolonial) texts.

2- Textual Analysis

A critic utilizing postcolonial theory should comb a text for examples of (a) colonialist agendas and ideologies and (b) colonial dynamics throughout the process of colonization (from initial encounters between colonizers and the colonized to postcolonial independence). This section highlights some major concepts that have attracted the attention of postcolonial theorists as examples of the above themes, which frequently emerge in colonial and postcolonial literary works. Let us, for the sake of simplicity, divide this section into two parts. First, we focus on broad ideological frameworks that set up colonial agendas and often reappear in most colonial literature. Next, we discuss issues recorded or raised in texts that can help us make sense of the different steps of colonial processes. This section has been entitled "Textual Analysis" to indicate what literary critics can learn by focusing on the text only. In later sections, we discuss methods that involve moving beyond the text itself.

2-1- Ideological Foundations of the Text

A comfortable point of entry into postcolonial critique of literature written about colonial experiences and texts that portray minoritized and racialized populations is an attempt to identify the main **ideological horizon** of the text, or in other words its **agenda**. When engaging with a text, a postcolonial critic should reflect on the work's stance on colonialism and imperialism and the agenda it proposes based on this stance. To simplify, the agenda could be (a) a **colonialist agenda**, (b) an **anti-colonialist agenda**, or (c) a **conflicted agenda**.

A colonialist agenda advocates colonialist ideologies, which justify or even encourage colonialism. **Eurocentrism** is the mother ideology of the doctrines stating that due to the "natural" superiority of the West, Western beliefs, and Western practices, colonialism is not only justified, it is also a favor to the colonized inasmuch as contact with white European culture will civilize populations with "backward" cultures. In contrast, an anti-colonialist agenda questions Eurocentrism, criticizes its components, and contributes to resistance movements against colonialism. Major Eurocentric doctrines are varied but include: exceptionalism of white societies, superiority of the white race, uniqueness of European reason and rationality, white man's knowledge and scientific advantage, white man's mission to conquer and transform the world, the moral and religious superiority of white man, and white man's civilizing presence.

Sometimes, however, texts might have conflicted agendas. "Conflicted" could mean random and disorganized with contradictory visions, but it could also indicate a **nuanced agenda** meant to encompass all the complexities of colonial experiences. A text may, for instance, picture the weaknesses of both the colonized and the colonizer. It might describe both sides' vulnerabilities, confusions, and errors in order to portray the process of colonialism rather than take sides. In postcolonial theory and black studies, it has been argued that a nuanced presentation of colonial processes can portray the struggles of the colonized in a more realistic way and thus could help create rational and sustainable decolonization dynamics. Providing guidelines on the creation of "an honest American Negro literature" in "The Negro Artist and The Racial Mountain" (1926), Langston Hughes, a celebrated African American writer of the Harlem Renaissance, held that the best kind of literature has a nuanced agenda. Quality literature, he argued, does not try to please a white or black audience. Instead, it objectively reflects the reality. Hughes' example of such an achievement is *Cane* (1923) by Jean Toomer, a novel in the form of a collection of free-standing vignettes that describe the experiences of African Americans in the United States. Hughes wrote:

> The Negro artist works against an undertow of sharp criticism and misunderstanding from his own group and unintentional bribes from the whites. "Oh, be respectable, write about nice people, show how good we are," say the Negroes. "Be stereotyped, don't go too far, don't shatter our illusions about you, don't amuse us too seriously. We will pay you," say the whites. Both would have told Jean Toomer not to write *Cane*. The colored people did not praise it. The white people did not buy it. Most of the colored people who did read *Cane* hate it. They are afraid of it. Although the critics gave it good reviews the public remained indifferent. Yet (excepting the work of Du Bois) *Cane* contains the finest prose written by a Negro in America. And like the singing of Robeson, it is truly racial. (From "The Negro Artist and The Racial Mountain")

Exemplifying the agendas of canonical literary works that can represent texts with colonialist or anti-colonialist agendas is difficult because agendas are always complex enough to be interpreted differently. However, with allowing some simplification required by an introductory pamphlet like this document, here are some examples. Joseph Rudyard Kipling's *Kim* (1901) has often been criticized as a work with a colonial agenda because of the portrayal of the Anglo-Indian characters in the novel, whose pride as members of the British Empire gives them perceived superiority over native

Indians. *A Passage to India* (1924) by Edward Morgan Forster, on the other hand, has often been described as having an anti-colonial agenda. The novel explores the artificiality and corruption of the British imperialists in India. Unlike these two works with *loaded* agendas, one can see more of a *conflicted* agenda in Josef Conrad's *Heart of Darkness* (1902) with a representation of a "primitive" Africa but at the same time revealing the barbaric nature of the "civilized" West. The story is told in a way where savagery and brutality cease to be the attributes of either side, as is often treated. Barbarism in the novel manifests itself beyond the people, white or black, and instead is written more as an outcome of certain historical, geographical, technological, and ideological circumstances. In this novel, colonialism is portrayed as more savage than the colonizer or the colonized. Conrad pictures colonialism as a machine that sooner or later will shred the lives of its participants regardless of which side they belong to.

The agendas suggested here in these works are by no means definite. They can be disputed by postcolonial critics depending on what lenses they use and what they emphasize in a text. It is important to remember that identifying a work's agenda is not the purpose of the conversation in postcolonial theory but its beginning. Nevertheless, thinking about the agenda of a text is a useful practice for emerging critics because it helps them read the work through its ideological foundations.

Throughout this text, each section will end with a question. Concluding theoretical topics with questions is intended to simplify and restate the arguments, and at the same time provide emerging critics with tangible guidelines. Here, for instance, is a question regarding the previous paragraphs:

2-1-1- Does the work have a colonialist agenda? Does the work have an anti-colonialist agenda? Does the work have a conflicted/nuanced agenda?

The agenda of a literary work is typically determined by an analysis of the major motifs of the work. Colonial literature hosts motifs that can be associated with uncomfortable historical experiences rooted in colonialism. While reflecting on the agenda of a piece of writing, a postcolonial critic should identify such motifs and decide what kind of agenda the presentation of these motifs reinforces. The following question lists some major motifs often employed in colonial literature:

> **2-1-2- Does the work discuss racism, ethnic identity, language, identity crisis, or racially motivated class differences and power struggle? Does the work depict cultural genocide (or cultural oblivion), immigration, deportation, slavery, lynching, and so on? Does it include the experiences of the disenfranchised, the marginalized, the unhomed, and the displaced? Does it picture oppressive regimes, native and minority resistance, rebellion, revolution, or civil war?**

In order to have a better understanding of a work's general tenor and tone, it is equally important that a critic asks what kind of image of the colonized and colonizers the work represents. We will later study in detail the stereotypes that colonizers construct to represent members of the "other" side in order to justify their exploitation and occupation. Here, however, we can broadly discuss the image of the characters in relation to a work's agenda. Let us for instance compare images of Africans portrayed in the following two passages. The first quote is from Joseph Conrad's *Heart of Darkness*, where Marlow, the main character, describes his impression of native workers:

> Six black men advanced in a file, toiling up the path. They walked erect and slow, balancing small baskets full of earth on their heads, and the clink kept time with their footsteps. Black rags were wound round

their loins, and the short ends behind wagged to and fro like tails. ... They were called criminals, and the outraged law, like the bursting shells, had come to them, an insoluble mystery from over the sea. All their meager breasts panted together, the violently dilated nostrils quivered, the eyes stared stonily uphill. They passed me within six inches, without a glance, with that complete, deathlike indifference of unhappy savages.

Now read the following poem "The Negro Speaks of Rivers" by Langston Hughes and compare the image of the poem's persona with Conrad's portrayal:

I've known rivers;
I've known rivers ancient as the world and older than the flow of human blood in human veins.
My soul has grown deep like the rivers.
I bathed in the Euphrates when dawns were young.
I built my hut near the Congo and it lulled me to sleep.
I looked upon the Nile and raised the pyramids above it.
I heard the singing of the Mississippi when Abe Lincoln went down to New Orleans, and I've seen its muddy bosom turn all golden in the sunset.

Whereas Conrad depicts the laboring black men as indifferent, ignorant, and actionless "unhappy savages" with "violently dilated nostrils" and filthy "rags ... round their loins," the Hughes' poetic character is a civilization building force and a source of wisdom. He transforms from man at the dawn of time into an Egyptian slave, a colonized African, and a slave in America. He has built human civilization phase by phase by his productive presence. He is a source of knowledge. His lived experience is our historic knowledge. He has inherited the knowledge of all the rivers. He is also hopeful. He knows things change. He has seen mud turn into gold. Langston Hughes' creation of the image of a liberated black slave recalling the past is a deliberate attempt to challenge the stereotypes fabricated by colonial white literature—stereotypes picturing men and women of color as savage, underdeveloped, ignorant, emotional, irrational, mistrustful, gullible, and decadent.

Thus, reflection on literary characters' image is another important question to help determine the broad attitude of a text and its agenda in colonial terms:

2-1-3- What image of the colonized and/or colonizers does the work offer? How can this depiction inform us about the ideological foundation of the text?

Colonialism and imperialism, in old and current forms, are often justified with discourses that normalize or even glorify the brutality involved in colonization — discourses such as the mission of the West to provide the rest of the world with "civilization," "progress," "freedoms," and ironically "peace." This form of justification is also accompanied by other arguments such as conversion of "the other" through missionarism, liberal human rights including white gender perceptions, and neoliberal free market strategies. Despite all justifications the main purpose of colonialism is always first and foremost material gain, be it the **occupation of land** or illegal **access to resources**. Examining colonial literature will highlight that the accumulation of wealth among privileged populations has been made possible because of appropriated land and resources. Hence, land occupation, resource appropriation, and economic exploitation are important themes and motifs to look for in a work and to highlight in critical conversations. Such analyses can also include the writer's attitude towards occupation and/or appropriation.

Among better known works, for instance, *The Color Purple* (1982) by Alice Walker and *Things Fall Apart* (1958) by Chinua Achebe have chapters intentionally describing economic dynamics caused by colonial contact and occupation. In other literary works, references to material gain could be less direct and be hidden between the lines beyond the conscious concern of the text. For instance, in the following lines from Alexander Pope's mock-heroic *The Rape of the Lock* (1712), while Pope's focus is on the superficiality of the eighteen century English aristocracy and the triviality of their everyday lives, the text—in the margins of the story—lists lines that list products brought back to the center of the empire for consumption. Read the following lines and note the make-up products and their origins. See how a critic can study these lines to map out colonialized territories and shed light on economic activities of the time:

> Unnumbered treasures ope at once, and here
> The various offerings of the world appear;
> From each she nicely culls with curious toil,
> And decks the goddess with the glittering spoil.
> This casket India's glowing gems unlocks,
> And all Arabia breathes from yonder box.

The use of the words "offering" and "spoil," with their religious and military connotations, reinforces the idea of a (militarily and ideologically) "superior" England devouring the resources of "inferior" lands. References to colonial experiences thus may not be the main focus of a work but be found in the margins of the text. As the final question in this opening section, which focused on the ideological foundation of a literary work, let us stress the importance of material profit and exploitation:

2-1-4- Does the work show that—despite racial, religious, or moral claims—material gain is the main goal of colonialism?

2-2- Colonization: Process and Dynamics

Whereas the questions discussed in the previous section were meant to help emerging critics identify the general orientation of a text and its stance on colonialism, this section offers a more nuanced look at the mechanisms of colonialism, its developmental patterns, and its consequences by introducing some of the concepts that have helped postcolonial thinkers make sense and articulate the processes involved in colonialism—concepts such as **contact, cultural heritage, othering, assimilation, mimicry, nativism, hybridity**, and so on.

To arrange these concepts in a logical order, one can think about them against the backdrop of a simplified sketch of the major steps colonization and imperialism involve. Schematically speaking, the first step in the process of colonization is contact: colonizers encounter an indigenous society and culture. As soon as colonizers enter the land, the indigenous culture is disturbed. When colonizers find their ground, they start propagating the idea that the colonized are different from them and colonizers' ways and beliefs are superior to those of the nations which originally owned the land. Imagining and painting indigenous populations as inferior is typically followed by occupying land and political space and consequently violence and discrimination against native populations. The locals resist. If resistance fails, indigenous culture is actively undermined or eradicated. As a result, the colonized start copying their colonizers' behavior, language, and lifestyle. Mimicry, however, won't provide equal status for the colonized. The colonized, having lost their identity, turn into outsiders—both in their own land and in the colonizers' home due to continued acts of racial discrimination and marginalization. As time passes and the technological and economic gap between colonizers and the colonized shrinks, independence is gained, often celebrated with revolutionary sentiments. Yet cultural revival and building ideal native societies might prove too difficult to achieve because of (a) neo-colonial sabotage and remote imperialism, (b) the corruption of new leaders, and (c) lack of compatibility between traditional cultural practices and current social, political, and economic circumstances. This challenge could result in disappointment, alienation, and double identity, all indicative of how complex decolonization dynamics could be and of the significant amount of patience, stamina, and creativity needed for healing and complete recovery.

The questions that follow unpack the steps highlighted in the above (simplified) sketch, starting with inquiry about the **pre-contact period**. Emerging postcolonial critics can look for textual evidence that helps better understanding of native cultures before encounters with colonizers were made. Literary texts are pieces of historical evidence. They tell us a great deal about beliefs, philosophies, traditions, social practices, rites and rituals, and so forth. It is important to unearth and re-examine pre-colonial cultural elements because they have usually been misunderstood, misinterpreted, misrepresented, or eradicated by colonizers and sometimes forgotten by the colonized. Thus, in reading a text a critic can look for traces of pre-contact indigenous culture, traditions, heritage, and history.

Although the best source for studying indigenous cultures is native nations' pre-contact texts (written and oral), there are also plenty of examples of such evidence in European literature. For instance, in the following passage from Daniel Defoe's *Robinson Crusoe* (1719), Robinson (the main character) reflects on Friday's (Robinson's native companion) religion—about which he has just learned through a brief conversation. Putting the literacy context of the novel aside, one can use the text to think about the religious practices of South American indigenous populations in the light of this evidence:

> He told me one day, that if our God could hear us up beyond the sun, He must needs be a greater god than their Benamuckee, who lived but a little way off, and yet could not hear till they never went up to the great mountains where he dwelt to speak to him. I asked him if ever he went thither to speak to him; he said no, they went that were young men; none went there but the old men.

This brief description, although biased, could be used as a piece of evidence next to other materials to help us make sense of this pre-contact religion. This short passage, for instance, tells us much about the structure of the religion (god, priesthood) and worshiping site and rights; it also provides linguistic references for further inquiry. Postcolonial critics, in the same manner, can catalog cultural practices, rites and rituals, religious beliefs, and social practices of an indigenous people revived from literary texts. While reading passages with historical content, emerging postcolonial critics can ask:

2-2-1- Can the work tell us anything about the pre-contact culture, beliefs, social practices, heritage, and history of an indigenous population?

Colonial invasion and subjugation of other cultures do not only happen because of military, technological, and economic superiority; they also require an ideological preparation through public discourse to encourage masses of people to take part in colonial atrocities. Occupation, theft, murder, and slavery are so vividly unethical that discourses are needed to justify these acts. Colonizers have to prove to themselves and to their fellow countrymen that their mistreatment of other people is justified. Remember that colonialism requires massive mobilization of forces, resources, and people including the clergy, academia, and the intelligentsia. Such mobilization indeed requires ideological readiness.

A vital part of justification for colonial aggression is **othering** or **otherizing**. Othering is a process by which colonizers create a sharp contrast between them and the colonized by picturing the colonized as inferior and subhuman. When one regards others as lower than human, they become convinced that ethical measures do not apply. That is why colonizers label racialized people with characteristics that show them as irrational, uncivilized, violent, and unintelligent. Othering is the fabrication of discourses of difference to create an illusion for subjugation of the other without a sense of guilt.

Eurocentric othering includes a long list of contrast making binary oppositions. They start with the oppositions that we often take for granted but develop into vocabulary soaked in hatred and aggression. They start with "us" and "them," "the self" and "the other," "black" and "white," and "the West" and "the Orient," and continue as "the evolved" and "the underdeveloped," "the civilized" and "the barbarians," "beautiful" and "ugly," "good" and "evil," "the moral" and "the immoral," "the faithful" and "the infidels," "the superior" and "the inferior," "the center" and "the periphery," and finally "the empire" and "the colonized."

In his influential book *Orientalism* (1978), Palestinian born American Edward Said demonstrates how Western historians, anthropologists, linguists, archaeologists, and politicians have "invented" the concept "Orient," a discourse propagated by the mass media and the entertainment industry. Analyzing how perceived non-Westerners are portrayed in literature and cultural products, Said wrote in *Orientalism*:

> Orientals or Arabs are thereafter shown to be gullible, "devoid of energy and initiative," much given to "fulsome flattery," intrigue, cunning and unkindness to animals; Orientals cannot walk on either a road or pavement (their disordered minds fail to understand what the clever European grasps immediately, that roads and pavements are made for walking); Orientals are inveterate liars, they are "lethargic and suspicious," and in everything oppose the clarity, directness, and nobility of the Anglo-Saxon race.

As an example of the invention of the Orient by Western writers, let us, after Edward Said's passage, read some lines by Charles Darwin. In this passage, from *The Descent of Man* (1871), Darwin describes the Fuegians, the inhabitants of Tierra del Fuego, as follows:

> The main conclusion arrived at in this work, namely that man is descended from some lowly-organized form, will, I regret to think, be highly distasteful to many persons. But there can hardly be a doubt that we are descended from barbarians. The astonishment which I felt

on first seeing a party of Fuegians on a wild and broken shore will never be forgotten by me, for the reflection at once rushed into my mind- such were our ancestors. These men were absolutely naked and bedaubed with paint, their long hair was tangled, their mouths frothed with excitement, and their expression was wild, startled, and distrustful. They possessed hardly any arts, and like wild animals lived on what they could catch; they had no government, and were merciless to everyone not of their own small tribe.

The "astonishment" with which naturalist Darwin, draws a thick line between "the self" and "the other" and demeans the Fuegians' appearance, culture, morality, and politics is also reflected in Anglo-American literary works. See how Charlotte Brontë's character Bertha Mason in *Jane Eyre* (1847) echoes the same mentality:

Fearful and ghastly to me ... It was a discoloured face—it was a savage face. I wish I could forget the roll of red eyes and the fearful blackened inflation of linaments.

And somewhere else in the book:

[A] figure ran backwards and forwards. What it was, whether beast or human being, one could not, at first sight, tell: it groveled ... on all fours, it snatched and growled like some strange wild animal ... .

Michiko Kakutani in a New York Times article entitled "Bigotry in Motion" (1997) captures the same tone and worldview that otherizes people of color as less than human, as "wild animals," in the poetry of T. S. Eliot:

In "March Hare," Eliot writes about a Negro, all "teeth and smile," and titles an interview with Booker T. Washington "Up From Possum Stew!" or "How I Set the Nigger Free!" One long, scatological poem features a sexually well-endowed black monarch named Bolo, who is attended by "a wild and hardy set of blacks" -- "an innocent and playful lot/But most disgusting dirty."

The act of othering, hence, prepares colonizers' consciousness for inhuman aggression, ironically in the name of humanity. It is important that emerging literary critics familiarize themselves with this concept and try to identify examples of othering in texts that they write about. It is important to ask:

2-2-2- Are there instances of othering (or otherizing) in the text?

Othering can happen in different forms. It can underline differences between "us" and "them" based on sex, gender, social status, religion, language, culture, ethnicity, race, and so on. Colonial othering has mainly fed on **Eurocentrism** as its ideological foundation. As briefly mentioned earlier, colonizers have used **discourses** such as security, morality, homogeneity, nationalism, racial superiority, civilization, modernity, rationality, science, progress, free trade, human rights, anti-terrorism, and alike arguments in order to justify their aggression. These **justifications** are usually constructed through a Eurocentric lens that presupposes the West as civilized, just, moral, righteous, and progressive and thus in a position to rule, judge, and punish others. A critic practicing postcolonial criticism should read works to identify such Eurocentric justifications.

Read, for instance, this passage from *Robinson Crusoe*, where Robinson evokes the Eurocentric belief in the superiority of white colonizers in terms of knowledge, truth, and religion to describe his interactions with Friday:

> From these things I began to instruct him in the knowledge of the true God. I told him that the great Maker of all things lived up there, pointing up towards heaven; that He governs the world by the same power and providence by which He had made it; that he was omnipotent, could do every thing for us, give every thing to us, take

every thing from us; and thus by degrees I opened his eyes.

An emerging postcolonial critic should always be vigilant for such Eurocentric justifications that indicate colonizers' self-image as superior humans with superior beliefs:

2-2-2- Does the work discuss any kind of justification for colonialism? Does it portray Eurocentrism or a Eurocentric sense of supremacy and superiority?

Western colonialism has historically had an obsession with race and racial difference. The same fixation is also prevalent in Western intelligentsia. For instance, Western academics over the past centuries have received enormous amount of funding to study "the other" to highlight differences in terms of cultural practices, linguistic features, intellectual performance, historical background, and so on. This so called "empirical research" has been mainly at the service of an act of othering that emphasizes the superiority of the European body and the "perfection" and "beauty" of physical features of white people, symbolic of their supremacy in general. As a reaction to this obsession with whiteness and "Caucasian" physical features, some postcolonial critics and black thinkers have written about the significance of how **racialized people's looks**, features, complexion, and color are portrayed in literature. As a result, the representation of the appearance of natives, or rather the degrading of native looks, has been of postcolonial interest. One should note that the belief in the "perfection" of the European body entails unmentioned connotations that go beyond pure aesthetics: "They do not look like us; we are more beautiful; so they can be flogged, lynched, displaced, enslaved, or bombed."

In the following lines from *Robinson Crusoe* see how indigenous features are demeaned and how resemblance to European looks is admired as a source of trust. Read how Robinson describes Friday's features:

> He had a very good countenance, not a fierce and surly aspect; but seemed to have something very manly in his face, and yet he had all the sweetness and softness of an European in his countenance too, especially when he smiled. His hair was long and black, not curled like wool; his forehead very high and large, and a great vivacity and sparkling sharpness in his eyes. The colour of his skin was not quite black, but very tawny; and yet not of an ugly yellow nauseous tawny, as the Brazilians, and Virginians, and other natives of America are, but of a bright kind of a dun olive colour, that had in it something very agreeable, tho' not very easy to describe.

A postcolonial critic should be sensitive about the manner in which racialized individuals are portrayed. Those passages should be extracted and critiqued. In contrast, there are also many examples of literary works where the physical features of minoritized populations are, more realistically, described in a positive light. Some postcolonial writers of color have also intentionally celebrated non-white physical features in a conscious response to the said obsession with whiteness and its corresponding physical attributes. Postcolonial critics could also highlight such texts. As an example, Langston Hughes in a poem called "Harlem Sweeties" celebrates what Daniel Defoe regards as "ugly" and "nauseous". These are the opening lines of "Harlem Sweeties":

> Have you dug the spill
> Of Sugar Hill[1]?
> Cast your gims
> On this sepia thrill:
> Brown sugar lassie,
> Caramel treat,
> Honey-gold baby

1- Sugar Hill is a section of Harlem where the more prosperous African Americans once lived.

Sweet enough to eat.
Peach-skinned girlie,
Coffee and cream,
Chocolate darling
Out of a dream.
Walnut tinted
Or cocoa brown
Pomegranate-lipped
Pride of the town.

As explained before, a focus on looks should not be considered a frivolous attempt since racialized populations often see such expressions of "sense of beauty" and "taste" in association with aggression, savagery, and discrimination. We will talk more about colonizers' savagery, but let us first review the question related to this section. When reading a text, ask:

2-2-3- How are aboriginal and racialized peoples' looks, physical features, complexion, and color portrayed in the work? Are they scorned as a source of inferiority? Is the writer dehumanizing native looks? Or alternatively, are the minorities pictured realistically? Is their beauty celebrated? Finally, how does the writer's view of people of colors' physique and also personality informs larger ideological themes in the work such as Eurocentrism and othering?

Regular othering and dehumanizing typically lead to aggression. The irony of the violence that follows othering is that the aggressor portrays the other as less than human only to perform savage oppression upon the colonized. In other words, justification through othering functions as guilt reduction for the aggressor's barbarism; it is a mechanism to project colonizers' savagery onto natives in the name of civility and progress. Colonizers' civilization, thus, is merely disguised savagery. Postcolonial writers have reported their experiences with this **civilized savagery**. In the following passage see how Minke, the native central character in Pramoedya Ananta Toer's *This Earth of Mankind* (1980), describes the same phenomenon. Minke is an intelligent Javanese boy who admires the modernity brought by the Dutch to the East Indies (today's Indonesia), but gradually realizes that the European man's modernity is only a form of savage oppression:

> All that glorified European science and learning was a load of nonsense, empty talk. Empty talk! In the end it all would be nothing more than a tool to rob us of all we loved, all we owned: honor, sweat, rights, even child and wife.
> … the words of my mother came back to me: "The Dutch are very, very powerful but they have never stolen people's wives as did the kings of Java." But now, Mother? It is none other than your own daughter-in-law they are threatening to steal, to steal a child from her mother, a wife from her husband; and they want, too, to steal the fruits of Mama's hard work and everything she has strived to achieve over the last twenty years without ever a holiday. And all this was based upon no more than beautiful documents written by expert scribes and clerks with their indelible black ink that soaked halfway through the thickness of the paper.

It is important that literary critics highlight acts of savagery performed by colonizers to crack the façade of "civility" and "progress" that colonizers claim to share with the world. Next to evidence that can be collected in white colonial literature, there are many texts written by postcolonial writers who have captured such inhuman episodes. It is important to highlight those experiences by emphasizing the fact that the process that starts in the name of rationality, morality, progress, civilization, and so forth, often ends with savagery. Here is a poem by Michael Harper as an example of minoritized and racialized writers' attempts to highlight such episodes:

American History

Those four black girls blown up
In that Alabama church[2]
Remind me of five hundred middle passage blacks[3],
In a net, under water
In Charleston harbor
So redcoats wouldn't find them.
Can't find what you can't see
can you?

Evidence of such brazen immorality can undermine discourses that support claims to moral superiority. Colonialism can lower humankind to despicable baseness, albeit sugarcoated in slogans such as "peace," "morality," and "security":

2-2-4- Does the work show that despite colonizers' claims to rationality, morality, progress, civilization, and so on, what the colonized received from white Europeans was often savagery?

It is important to remember that colonialism does not function entirely on acts of primitive barbarism. Colonial rule, especially once established, tends to spread its tentacles through economic, scientific, educational, legal, and cultural channels. Let's not forget that the British, famously, colonized India through business entities, most importantly, the British East India Company, as well as military aggression. Emerging postcolonial critics should look for legal, academic, economic, and cultural structures that strengthen the hegemony of colonial rule—sometimes supported by the locals themselves because of their trust in colonizers' scientific superiority, for example, or their financial benefit thanks to the colonizers' presence.

---

[2] By a white racist as reprisal against 1960s civil-rights demonstrations.
[3] Captured, an en route from Africa to be sold as slaves.

Literary works often contain examples of this kind of more insipid colonialism. These examples include basic and overt forms of **cultural dominance**—like Robinson teaching English to Friday in *Robinson Crusoe*. There are also more sophisticated forms of colonial intervention such as neo-imperial **economic colonialism**. *Bamako*, a 2006 film directed by Abderrahmane Sissako, is a moving account of the role of the World Bank and the International Monetary Fund in economic struggles of less prosperous African countries. The film depicts the European financial interference in Africa, presented as economic aid, which has resulted in corruption and economic misfortune for local vulnerable populations.

Thus, in addition to a focus on manifestation of colonialism in overt violent acts, one should also ask:

2-2-5- Does the work discuss forms of legal, economic, or cultural colonialism?

The colonized are never a monolithic mass. Different colonized peoples—and also racialized and minoritized groups—are impacted by colonialism and racism differently. Feminist postcolonial writers, for instance, have emphasized the fact that colonized, racialized, and minoritized women are typically under **double pressure** compared with men because they have to deal with both racial discrimination and sexual oppression. Women are doubly silenced and doubly exploited, so they have a larger share of colonial savagery than many other social groups. Women of color have not only been exploited by white people for their labor, they have also been sexually abused. Additionally, some women of color are discriminated against even within their own communities as a result of patriarchal structures.

Among the texts we have discussed so far, two could be again mentioned with vivid themes of double pressure on women of color during the process of colonization and racialization. The main character in Alice Walker's *The Color Purple* is a black woman called

Celie. Although the book's larger theme could be described as racial oppression in the United Stated, and how African-Americans, have coped with it, because the story focuses on Celie, the book captures the experiences of women in the face of racial oppression. The book opens with the uncomfortable relationship between Celie and her father, Alphonso. Alphonso constantly beats and rapes Celie, his own daughter. This poisonous relationship even leads to two pregnancies. It is important for a postcolonial critic to underline such experiences and discuss socioeconomic and political circumstances that bred such behavior, where women of color can also fall victim to their own communities or even family members.

The second example is a character called Nyai Ontosoroh in *This Earth of Mankind* by Pramoedya Ananta Toer. In a common colonial practice in the East Indies, very young Nyai becomes a Dutch colonizer's concubine. Nyai is sold to the Dutchman by her father for a petty career promotion in the white master's business. Her position as a concubine turns Nyai into an underage sex slave with no legal rights whatsoever for claiming anything from the relationship, not even the children she has with the master. Here is how in the novel Nyai describes the trauma she experienced as a child:

> Father and mother went home in the same carriage. I was left on the chair, bathing in my own tears, shaking and not knowing what I must do. The world seemed dark. Looking up from under my bowed head, my vision blurred, I could still see Tuan Besar Kuasa as he entered the house after having said farewell to my parents. He picked up my suitcase and took it into a room. He came out of the room and approached me. He pulled my hand, ordering me to stand. I trembled. It wasn't that I didn't want to stand up, or that I was rebelling against an order. I didn't have the strength to stand. My kain was soaking with sweat. My legs trembled so badly, it was as if my bones and sinews had come loose from their joints. He picked me up as if I were an old pillow, carried me in his arms into the room, and put me down on a beautiful, clean bed, powerless. I was not able even to sit. I rolled over; perhaps I fainted.

Before we close this section, let us also read the following poem by Audre Lorde as another example of the sufferings of women of color recorded in literature:

Who Said It Was Simple

There are so many roots to the tree of anger
that sometimes the branches shatter
before they bear.
Sitting in Nedicks
the women rally before they march
discussing the problematic girls
they hire to make them free.
An almost white counterman passes
a waiting brother to serve them first
and the ladies neither notice nor reject
the slighter pleasures of their slavery.
But I who am bound by my mirror
as well as my bed
see causes in color
as well as sex

and sit here wondering
which me will survive
all these liberations.

Feminist postcolonial theory could also inspire attention to other minority social groups. Highlighting double pressure, one can similarly ask questions about the impact of colonialism on native and non-white LGBTQ+ communities, or social groups of different faiths, cultures, and languages. The same also could be investigated about people of mixed indigenous and Euro-American ancestry. Hence, the question for this section could be:

2-2-6- Does the work show how colonized women, and

women of color in general, are under double pressure? What about other minority social groups? Does the work show how minorities within minority groups are doubly oppressed or exploited as a result of colonialism?

When colonial rule is established and colonizers attempt to solidify their cultural hegemony, cultural interactions and frictions between the dominant group and minority populations can lead to complex forms of **cultural antagonism** or **cultural merger**. After a racial, ethnic, or religious group has established its dominance, conversations will rise regarding how the minoritized need to co-exist with the current reality. Based on circumstances, minority groups might engage with a range of options from **assimilation** to **cultural co-existence** and to **separatism**. This cultural ebb and flow is not typically fixed but fluid, and the way that the colonized perceive their status would impact their approach to the dominant group's culture differently at different points of the colonial process.

It is important to note that although dominant groups tend to eradicate the customs, traditions, language, art, and literature of the minoritized, oppressors are not by any means immune to cultural influence from the other side. Colonizers, for instance, have often enjoyed the hospitality of the colonized upon arrival on their lands and taken advantage of their traditional diet and medicine, and also of the locals' knowledge of the land and its resources. Among different topics regarding this cultural tension and interaction, there are two concepts that frequently appear in postcolonial thought and thus require the attention of emerging postcolonial critics: **cultural appropriation** and **subaltern culture**.

Despite claims to cultural superiority, native art and culture have often been used, regulated, and adopted by colonizers for entertainment and financial gain. Non-white cultural practices have been copied, rebranded, commodified, and commercialized by dominant groups in different forms of cultural appropriation.

Aboriginal non-white cultures are considered inferior until they are adopted by the dominant group for artistic, political, or financial purposes. It is important that critics point out the contradictory nature of cultural appropriation when they encounter instances of this dishonest cultural practice.

Another interesting form of analysis is reflection on the life and experiences of the **subaltern**. The concept "subaltern" has had a long and complex history in the field of postcolonial studies, and thus it is a difficult term to define. For our purposes in this introductory pamphlet though, let us imagine the subaltern as a low-level member of the sub-divisions of a social hierarchy. The subaltern, in this sense, could be viewed as lower-rank colonizers in the margins of the empire. Alternatively, the subaltern could be a native alienated because of his social status (or race, gender, ...) and thus lacking voice and agency within the native population. It is important for a postcolonial critic to pay attention to subaltern characters and analyze their cultural existence and transformations in interactions occurring in the course of colonial aggression. Studying the subaltern population can provide nuanced insights into cultural realities of colonial life since members of the subaltern class avoid the cultural hegemony of the colonized and also organized native cultural backlash. In a sense, the subaltern's cultural life can potentially represent organic cultural dynamics and tendencies in a territory struggling with racial and consequently cultural tensions.

Keeping possible complexities such as cultural appropriation and the subaltern in mind, let us return to the broader themes of the section, namely cultural merger and antagonism. As an example of how frequently the question of culture appears in literature, let us read "Theme for English B" by Langston Hughes. The poem a classic example in the context of the United States, which is still largely segregated with sometimes sharp cultural and socioeconomic contrasts between white and African-American populations. One popular interpretation of the poem is that Hughes delicately pictures the development of a cultural merger and advocates cultural tolerance and co-existence despite a bitter history in the background.

The instructor said,

> *Go home and write*
> *a page tonight.*
> *And let that page come out of you---*
> *Then, it will be true.*

I wonder if it's that simple?
I am twenty-two, colored, born in Winston-Salem.
I went to school there, then Durham, then here
to this college on the hill above Harlem.
I am the only colored student in my class.
The steps from the hill lead down into Harlem
through a park, then I cross St. Nicholas,
Eighth Avenue, Seventh, and I come to the Y,
the Harlem Branch Y, where I take the elevator
up to my room, sit down, and write this page:

> *It's not easy to know what is true for you or me*
> *at twenty-two, my age. But I guess I'm what*
> *I feel and see and hear, Harlem, I hear you:*
> *hear you, hear me---we two---you, me, talk on this page.*
> *(I hear New York too.) Me---who?*
>
> *Well, I like to eat, sleep, drink, and be in love.*
> *I like to work, read, learn, and understand life.*
> *I like a pipe for a Christmas present,*
> *or records---Bessie, bop, or Bach.*
> *I guess being colored doesn't make me NOT like*
> *the same things other folks like who are other races.*
> *So will my page be colored that I write?*
> *Being me, it will not be white.*
> *But it will be*
> *a part of you, instructor.*
> *You are white---*
> *yet a part of me, as I am a part of you*
> *That's American.*
> *Sometimes perhaps you don't want to be a part of me.*

Nor do I often want to be a part of you.
But we are, that's true!
As I learn from you,
I guess you learn from me---
although you're older---and white---
and somewhat more free.

This is my page for English B.

Let us sum up this section with the following question:

2-2-7- Does the work present examples of cultural merger or cultural antagonism? Does the text advocate assimilation, separatism, or cultural tolerance? Does it talk about indigenous cultural influence on colonizers despite their cultural dominance?

At the peak of colonial dominance, the colonized are either convinced or coerced to accept the superiority of the dominant group's values and way of life. At this point in the colonial process, the colonized are likely to adopt the rulers' belief sets and life style either as a survival strategy or even out of admiration for the ruling population that they view as "winners". The desire to **assimilate** into the dominant culture is usually hoped to be fulfilled by **mimicry**. To be welcomed and appreciated by the colonizers, the colonized try to copy their social practices, behavior, speech, dress code, and appearance.

Nevertheless, mimicry, will not breed respect and recognition, and the colonized soon realize that they will never be treated as equals. Notions that are meant to encourage people of color to behave "white" for success or survival are problematic because they are based on the racist idea that define aboriginals or people of color as lacking. Mimicry, hence, is only some form of cosmetic surgery, failing to impact the underlying racism whose main goal is still exploitation of labor and resources.

Even when mimicry helps some members of minoritized groups enter white spheres of power and influence, they are regarded as exceptions or exceptional individuals different from the "inferior" reality of their communities. Sometimes also, the projected success of those exceptions is consciously designed to create an image of diversity in a practice of **tokenism** as a political or marketing strategy. In the process of colonization and racialization, minoritized people, sooner or later, realize that mimicry will actually yield very little and is promoted by "masters" as a delaying strategy to avoid sharing power. Colonizers are very generous when it comes to sharing their belief systems and life style, yet they are parsimonious when sharing privilege is involved. That is why mimicry will typically lead to disappointment, disillusionment, and indignation.

A postcolonial critic can highlight examples of mimicry in literary works to help others make better sense of the phenomenon of mimicry and the complexities it involves. To give an example, Pramoedya Ananta Toer opens his novel *This Earth of Mankind* by describing how his main character, a native called Minke, has become attached to European education and learning brought by Dutch colonizers to Java (in today's Indonesia). Minke is one of very few native students of a Dutch school in Java who has been able to enter the school partly because of his perceived exceptional talent and partly because of the wealth and influence of his father, a Javanese local statesman. At the beginning of the novel, Minke expresses a strong belief in European modernity and is pleased with his access to European thought and manners:

> … I had never been to Europe, so I did not know if the director was telling the truth or not. But because it pleased me, I decided to believe him. And further, all my teachers had been born and educated in Europe. It didn't feel right to distrust my teachers. My parents had entrusted me to them. Among the educated European and Indo communities, they were considered to be the best teachers in all of the Netherlands Indies. So I was obliged to trust them.
>
> This science and learning, which I had been taught at school and

which I saw manifested in life all around me, meant that I was rather different from the general run of my countrymen.

Despite his talent and mastery of the Dutch language and European knowledge and, at the same time, his genuine desire to be an equal member of the ruling community, Minke, in the course of the novel, matures enough to realize that no matter how hard he tries, he can never beat the systematic racism inherent in the colonial structure through merit. Minke learns bitterly that some are simply "more equal than the other." Toward the end of the book, Minke and his mother-in-law, who is also a native, should appear in a court of law as a result of a number of incidents. Apart from the details of the case, this experience wakes Minke up to the fact that justice and rule of law are empty expressions that will never apply to non-Europeans:

> How can a court, and a European court too, manned by very educated people, experienced in matters of justice, with the degree of Bachelor of Laws, carry out the law this way, so opposed to our sense of law? Our sense of justice?
>
> "I didn't even get on to talking about the division of the property. Yes, indeed, even though the land was bought in my name, I don't have enough documentation to prove to a European court of law that the company itself is my property. All I tried to do was to defend Annelies [her daughter and Minke's wife, who is mixed race]. ... The judge said you are a Native, you have no business with this court." Mama grimaced angrily.
>
> "In the end," she added in a soft voice, "the issue is always the same: European against Native, against me. Remember this well: It is Europe that swallows up Natives while torturing us sadistically. .... Eu-r-ope.... only their skin is white," she swore. "Their hearts are full of nothing but hate."
>
> "And the attorney, he is a European too, Mama?"
>
> "Just a slave to money. The more money you give him, the more honest he is with you. That's Europe."
>
> I shuddered. Years and years of schooling were overturned in me with just three short sentences of a nyai (his mother-in-law, a native

concubine).

A literary critic could study cases such as Minke's experiences to provide detailed analysis of complexities of minoritized people's identity negotiation when being dominated by other cultures. So let us add this question to highlight the importance of mimicry in the process of colonization:

2-2-8- Are there any examples of mimicry in the text? What is your analysis of the dynamics of mimicry as narrated in the text? What sociocultural circumstances encourage mimicry? Can characters who lend themselves to assimilation achieve what they have been promised?

Colonialism has a certain life span as ruling by oppression cannot continue forever. Systematic segregation and discrimination will eventually create acts of **resistance**. In the following poem, see how Langston Hughes pictures the augmentation of oppressed populations' disappointment and outrage at discrimination, and warns about an ultimate explosion:

Harlem

What happens to a dream deferred?

Does it dry up
Like a raisin in the sun?
Or fester like a sore—
And then run?
Does it stink like rotten meat?
Or crust and sugar over—
Like a syrupy sweet?

Maybe it just sags
Like a heavy load.

Or *does it explode?*

Resistance will also eventually lead to **decolonization**: the unwilling withdrawal of colonizers from their colonies and the acquisition of independence by a former colony. Postcolonial thinkers have frequently used literature to learn about different forms of anti-colonial resistance, their roots, their dynamics, the challenges involved, strategies, failures and shortcomings, and also victories. Literary texts then become an important source of information about the histories of anti-colonial resistance.

Anti-colonial resistance, when used as subject matter of a literary work, can host a variety of themes such as cultural resistance, subversive social action, civil disobedience, negative resistance, strikes, demonstrations, riots, rebellion, guerrilla warfare, civil war, and revolution. It is important that postcolonial critics highlight these themes and analyze their different aspects.

Nil Darpan (The Indigo Mirror) is a Bengali play written by Dinabandhu Mitra and published, under a pseudonym, in 1860. The play is an artistic representation of a farmer movement against the British rule. During this protest, which was against indigo planters known as *Nil Vidroha* (Indigo Revolt), the farmers refused to plant indigo to attract attention to the pressures they were under. In an attempt to make sense of the movement, Indian scholar Sudipto Chatterjee writes:

> *Nildarpan*, contrary to popular belief, is hardly the revolutionary "protest" play it is championed to be. And although its invective is ostensibly directed against British indigo-plantation owners, the political schema of the plot owes more to middle-class conceptions of rebellious behavior rather than the organized, though unsuccessful, subaltern uprising that the indigo movement of 1860 actually had been. The peasant characters of the play display more urban *babu*-like behavioral attributes than anything else. The *babu* characters in the play, on the contrary, are much more convincingly portrayed. The play

on the whole acts out a middle-class fantasy of rebellion (that can only be realized on stage) and the *babu*'s social anxiety. *Nildarpan* set a precedent. More plays of so-called social protest, a large number of them in the *darpan* (or mirror-)style, began to follow suit; plays that purported to hold up a mirror, as it were, to the ills of society. Most notable among them were Mir Masarraf Hossain's *Jamida-darpan* (The Mirror of the Landowner, 1873), which was about a peasant rebellion against the land-owning babus, *Ca-Kar-Darpan* (The Tea-Planter's Mirror, 1875), by Daksinaranjan Cattopadhyay, that dealt with the poor working conditions at the British tea-estates in North Bengal and *Jel-darpan* (The Mirror of the Prison, 1876) that dealt with the terrible life of prisoners in the jail houses of Bengal, also by Daksinaranjan Cattopadhyay. All three plays protested the atrocities meted out by colonial agencies of domination, not to the urban middle class, but to the subaltern of subalterns--the rural working class majority of Bengal. Obviously, all of the plays raked the ire of the British and even some prominent members of the Bengali intellectual elite. (from "Performing (Domi-)Nation: Aspects of Nationalism in Nineteenth-Century Bengali Theatre")

Similarly, emerging postcolonial critics can study literature to discuss resistance and protest movements that started or strengthened decolonization processes:

2-2-9- Does the work portray any form of anti-colonial resistance? Can the text tell us what the people demanded—for example, political independence, civil rights, economic progress, wage increase, education, and so on? Does the work picture decolonization, or withdrawal and weakening of colonial forces and their local allies?

Political decolonization is frequently accompanied by a strong desire to discover and revive a lost cultural past. This desire is typically colored by nostalgia for a purely indigenous pre-colonial society. As decolonization progresses, native customs, traditions, manners, and values come to the fore, and outside influences are criticized and sometimes swept away. Political decolonization often occurs with a process of cultural purification. This process is referred to as **nativism**.

The connection between political independence and cultural decolonization impacts literature and text production immensely; it usually creates different forms of **literary self-definition**: an indigenous literature written by the natives and about the native land/nation. Postcolonial literature has produced a lot of works with **nativist agendas**. Writers of such literature work to reject colonial ideology and **reclaim** their native past. They remember and glorify their traditional ways. They celebrate who they are, what they have, and what they look like. An example of the rise of nativism could be the Negritude Movement in France in the 1930s. The movement, which was influenced by the Harlem Renaissance, was to establish a common black identity and reject French colonial racism.

In terms of literature, the case of *One Hundred Years of Solitude* (1967) by Colombian novelist Gabriel Garcia Marquez would be an interesting example as there has been much conversation about nativist elements in this work. Employing *magic realism*, Marquez showcases a myriad of native traditions, social practices, anecdotes, and philosophies in his novel. For instance, there are characters in the novel that return from the dead. Fortunetelling is presented as an important source of knowledge. Magic is not treated as an extraordinary phenomenon and instead functions as a normal part of everyday life. Traditional tales and wisdom are invoked all through the book. Characters resemble mythical heroes. History, and accordingly the story, is not linear but cyclical. The significance of traditional practices in *One Hundred Years of Solitude* has been discussed in many publications. You, for instance, can read "Magic Realism As Post-Colonial Discourse" (1988) by Stephen Slemon to further study magic realism in the context of postcolonial cultures.

From another perspective, Wendy B. Faris, in "The Question of the Other: Cultural Critiques of Magical Realism" (2002), problematizes magic realism and doubts if the literary style is an effective strategy to genuinely value native traditions. Faris argues that the attention that the West has paid to magic realism is partly the continuity of the colonial mentality that sees the other as strange, mysterious, and exotic:

> The status of magical realism, its widespread popularity, and the critical use of the term are the subject of debate because at the same time that it is acknowledged by some as a significant decolonizing style, permitting new voices and traditions to be heard within the mainstream, it is denigrated by others as a commodifying kind of primitivism that, like the Orientalism analyzed by Edward Said and his successors, relegates colonies and their traditions to the role of cute, exotic psychological fantasies—visions of the colonizer's ever more distant, desirable, and/or despised self projected onto colonized others. (p. 101)

These examples can hopefully show some of the complexities of presenting indigenous traditions and social practices in literary works. While examining the concepts of anti-colonial resistance and decolonization in a literary work, a critic should also look for examples of cultural reclamation of the pre-colonial past:

2-2-10- Does the work advocate nativism and/or nationalism? Does the text invoke native traditions, mythology, religions, folklore, tales, social practices, and philosophies?

Historical cases show that successful decolonization and effective nativism might prove more challenging than initially imagined and postcolonial nations may not achieve complete political and cultural independence after the physical withdrawal of colonizers. Creating a **national consciousness** based on a pure pre-contact past might never be achieved. In their return to their native roots, postcolonial populations would typically see that cultural contact has changed their cultural trajectory to a degree that some of their traditions have become invisible, lost, and even irrelevant. They might find that their cultural reality now is a mix of their native heritage and the culture of the **empire** and its **mother country**. This mixed identity, **double consciousness, double vision,** or **hybridity**, typically results in cultural confusion and anxiety in the wake of independence. Hybridity can trigger feelings of **alienation** and **unhomeliness**, which have appeared in literary works as themes such as **hyphenated existence** and **symbolic return** (partial and cosmetic reconstruction of an imaginary native home).

Before discussing the next major challenge in the process of cultural revival, let us read again the following lines from "Theme for English B" by Langston Hughes to see how the persona of the poem admits to living a mixed identity:

> I guess being colored doesn't make me NOT like
> the same things other folks like who are other races.
> So will my page be colored that I write?
> Being me, it will not be white.
> But it will be
> a part of you, instructor.
> You are white---
> yet a part of me, as I am a part of you.
> That's American.

2-2-11- Does the work host themes such as hybridity, double consciousness, double vision, unhomeliness, or symbolic return?

Next to struggles with double identity after independence (or in a post-segregation period as exemplified in the above poem), postcolonial societies also learn that colonialism is tenacious and despite the physical withdrawal of colonial political and military forces, emerging structures might not function as well as had been hoped. Postcolonial experiences show that after colonial rulers let go of power, they could be replaced with corrupt native elites who occupy the same white systems, designed for control and oppression. *Xala* is a 1975 film directed by Senegalese director Ousmane Sembène. The film is a critique of post-independence African governments and their failures. The film, based on Sembène's novel with the same title, comically centers around the erectile dysfunction of a successful businessman, El Hadji, upon his marriage with his third wife. El Hadji's impotence is a metaphoric depiction of the incompetence of African postcolonial native governments of the time.

Furthermore, before handing over the political power, former colonizers—or dominant populations in post-civil rights movements—create economic and institutional networks that could direct the resources of their former colonies back into their control even long after their departure. This last stage of imperialism is usually referred to as **neocolonialism**. Neocolonial measures include a large range of activities such as creating fake countries with no historical background, supporting puppet governments and leaders, sponsoring terrorism to undermine independent governments, funding coup d'etat and regime change, and launching different forms of cultural invasion. Neocolonialism also actively engages with running international organizations and monetary systems that can cripple independent countries through economic sanctions, backbreaking loans, and debt. Examples of these multinational organizations include the World Bank, the International Monetary Fund, and the World Trade Organization. Similarly, on the cultural front there are institutions such as the Organisation Internationale la Francophonie, and the British Council, which promote cultural and linguistic imperialism. And in sports, International Olympic Committee (IOC) and The Fédération Internationale de Football Association (FIFA) are a few examples.

An emerging literary critic can read literary works to examine minoritized peoples' experiences with different forms of neocolonialism. Bamako (2006) is a film made by Mauritanian director Abderrahmane Sissako. The film depicts a trial in Bamako, the capital of Mali. In the court the two sides debate the role of the World Bank and International Monetary Fund. The African attorneys argue that these institutions are mainly guided by special interest. It is argued that corruption and mismanagement of these organizations have rendered African and other developing countries financially desperate, while these international bodies were supposed to be at the service of development and prosperity. Here are some lines from the exchanges in the court from the film:

> Yes Mr. President, this is precisely a disease that is organized and administered, and structured, and injected into a people. This is the cynicism of debt; the vicious circle of debt. This debt that has completely destroyed our economy and sucked up all our vitality to the point that we cannot finish paying our debt. What can one do in the face of the violence of this debt? I have learned from Latin America. They tell us, "*la deuda es impagable*"; that the debt is simply unpayable. Yes Mr. President, it is unpayable because it's illegitimate. It is unpayable because it is violent. It is unpayable because it's just all of these together. It is unsustainable. Let us add to the violence of the debt, the brokenness of our public service and our social service …

So the question to keep in mind regarding continuing control in the postcolonial period could be:

2-2-12- How does the work discuss neocolonialism? Are there examples of corrupt or puppet regimes following in the footsteps of colonizers? What neo-imperial methods are portrayed in the text; for instance, are there examples of destructions caused by global capitalism, corporate industrialization, monetary funds, international banks, European cultural organizations, and Western academic centers?

The above question closes the present section, which makes up the largest proportion of this pamphlet. The topics discussed in this section were major concepts frequently referred to and employed by postcolonial thinkers. The concepts here were organized according to a simplified timeline of the progression of colonization from pre-contact to postcolonial periods.

The literary analysis based on these concepts will take the form of content-based study of literary (or academic and artistic) texts. This focus on content, however, does not mean that postcolonial theorists have not paid attention to form or aesthetics. There have also been conversations about publishing and dissemination of literary works. In what follows, we briefly discuss those issues.

3- Language and Form

Empires seek to standardize the territories they colonize for smoother management of money and resources. Part and parcel of the standardization imposed by Western colonialism has been the eradication of the cultural identity of colonized populations. It is no accident that Christian missionaries have been a significant component of European colonialism as the empire's cultural army. One important edge of cultural colonialism is the imposition of the language of the mother country and pushing native languages away from social, political, academic, educational and legal interactions. This **linguistic imperialism** has typically created much hurt and humiliation, and thus much sensitivity about language and language use. Part of this linguistic harm has been caused by the disappearance of texts (written and oral) in indigenous and minority languages, leading to loss of traditional literature, mythologies, philosophies, and knowledge. On the other hand, however, joining a larger linguistic club has given native literary works written in European languages the chance to be read by a wider readership. Also, colonies have created their own distinct versions of the language of the empire enriched by context-specific histories and experiences. Take English for example. The word "Englishes" has been used to more precisely reflect variant manifestations of the English language such as South African English, Indian English, Pakistani English and so on.

The complexity of the issue of language hence has always put writers from minority populations in a very difficult position. They constantly debate if they should write in their native languages or the dominant language imposed on them by historical power relations. This tension could be the focus of a postcolonial literary critic, both as the subject matter of a particular work or as the analysis of the trajectory of a writer—or even the languages used in an intellectual or literary movement. Previously, we have made references to *This Earth of Mankind* by Pramoedya Ananta Toer for examples of postcolonial concepts. Here is another passage from the same book to illustrate the preoccupation of postcolonial writers with whether or not to use adopted European languages. Minke is a talented native boy who is attending a Dutch school in Java. He has received some attention as an up-and-coming writer, publishing pieces in local magazines. This passage is from a letter by his mother, a Javanese royal:

> I hear from those who read the Dutch papers that you have become a man of letters. Oh, Gus, why do you compose in a language that your mother cannot understand? Write the story of your love in the poetry of your ancestors so that your mother and the whole community may sing them.

If we look at English as an example of an imposed colonial language, postcolonial and racialized writers have reacted to using English in writing in three ways. A group of writers decided to write in English, arguing that the only way to be heard and noticed in a world dominated by European culture and literary tradition was to use European languages. Another group, in contrast, rejected English. For instance, Kenyan writer Ngugi wa Thiong'o (James Ngugi) wrote in his native Kikuyu language and then translated his own work into English. Writing in native languages was considered an important strategy to challenge colonial cultural influence. A third group decided to write in *their own* English. For instance, Salman Rushdi, in his *Midnight's Children* (1981), used a hybrid language of English and frequent appearances of Indian terms and concepts. In the context of minoritized writers, African-Americans in the US, for instance, successfully created a literature in their own black vernaculars. A critic can study a writer's attitude towards the colonial language by examining his or her prose and trajectory:

3-1- What does the literary trajectory of a postcolonial writer tell us about his or her attitude towards adopted European languages? Does he or she write in an adopted European language or in his or her native language or vernacular? As for a particular work in a native language or vernacular, how has this choice changed the tone of the work or the quality of poetics or storytelling, compared with mainstream Eurocentric literature? Has adopting the local language influenced the structure of the work and literary techniques used in the work?

The question of how to diversify the languages used in mainstream literature always goes hand in hand with a concern about native aesthetics, literary genres, and artistic forms—as also indicated by the last question above: "Has adopting the local language influenced the structure of the work or literary techniques?" Literary and formal elements can indeed be a space for resistance in the process of decolonization. Examples of how writers have employed formal elements to provide voice and presence for minoritized and racialized people include: Letting characters of color narrate the story, choosing geographical settings and imagery significant in non-white histories and traditions, transforming Eurocentric literary forms and genres, generating irregular forms as a form of rebellion against the established aesthetic hierarchy, challenging structured European prose by employing fragmented, genre-hybrid and multilingual texts, and juxtaposing white and native artistic traditions.

As well as challenging dominant European composition and rhetoric, the ultimate goal of restructuring mainstream genres is the creation of indigenous forms of expression based on artistic and cultural traditions undermined or eradicated by colonialism—creation of literary forms rooted in aboriginal dance, music, narration, religion, and carnivals. African American thinkers, for instance, believe that great African American literature formally borrows from the slave narrative, the oral tradition of black preaching, trash talk, jokes, folk tales, and, most importantly, the blues. African American writer Houston A. Baker JR in his *Blues, Ideology, and Afro-American Literature: A Vernacular Theory* (1984) writes:

> ... Afro-American culture is a complex, reflective enterprise which finds its proper figuration in blues conceived as a matrix. ... Afro-American blues constitute such a vibrant network. ... They are the multiplex, enabling script in which Afro-American discourse is inscribed.

Next, he continues to give examples of "blues moments in Afro-American expression":

> The expressive instances that I have in mind occur in passages such as the conclusion of the *Narrative of the Life of Fredrick Douglass.* Standing at a Nantucket convention, riffing (in the "break" suddenly confronting him) on the personal troubles he has seen and successfully negotiated in a "prisonhouse of American bondage," Douglass achieves a profoundly dignified blues voice. Zora Neale Houston's protagonist Janie in the novel *Their Eyes Were Watching God*—as she lyrically and idiomatically relates a tale of personal suffering and triumph that begins in the sexual exploitations of slavery—is a blues artist par excellence. Her wisdom might well be joined to that of Amiri Baraka's Walker Vessels (a "locomotive container" of blues?), whose chameleon code-switching from academic philosophy to blues insight makes him a veritable incarnation of the absorptively vernacular. The narrator of Richard

Wright's *Black Boy* inscribes a black blues life's lean desire and suggests yet a further instance of the matrix's expressive energies. Ellison's *Invisible Man* and Bakara's narrator in *The System of Dante's Hell* (whose blues book produces dance) provide additional examples. Finally, Toni Morrison's Milkman Dead in *Song of Solomon* discovers through "Sugarman's" song that an awesomely expressive blues response may well consist of improvisational and serendipitous surrender to the air . . . .

In their attempts to resist the dominance of Anglo-American rhetoric, minoritized writers have also tried to blur and broaden mainstream genres. *Borderlands/La Frontera: the New Mestiza* (1987) by Gloria Anzaldúa is a semi-autobiographical work of multi-genre prose and poetry passages. This book, as its title suggests, highlights various forms of invisible borders that exist in numerous opposing groups: Latinx and whites, men and women, heterosexuals and homosexuals, etc. The prose section of the book outlines a short history of the people who have inhabited the Mexico region, beginning with the oldest known inhabitants of what is now the United States and ending in the present day. The poetry section includes several poems centered on the theme of borders. In a more recent publication titled *Decolonizing Academia: Poverty, Oppression and Pain* (2018), Clelia O. Rodríguez employs a poetic academic rhetoric which stands in contrast with mainstream North American academic prose. She uses polemics, multiple languages, multiple genres, and alternative forms of academic citation.

Form, style, and aesthetics, thus, can be interesting areas for investigation for postcolonial critics. By highlighting non-European rhetorics and aesthetics, a critic would not only explore and explain what writers have created, but they could actively take part in constructing indigenous forms and stylistics. When reading a text, it is important to ask:

3-2- Have the formal elements of the text given minoritized characters more voice and presence? Has the writer

managed to create an alternative style, perhaps borrowing from indigenous aesthetics?

4- Readership and the Canon

Postcolonial literary criticism sometimes assumes a reader-response stance; meaning, it examines the position of readers in relation to the work or studies readers' interpretations of it. In other words, postcolonial critics are not only interested in the content of indigenous, colonial, and postcolonial literatures, but also how readers received literary works, and how their aesthetic appraisal of the works changed over time. They, for instance, have often been occupied with conversations about **the canon**, or literary works selected and recognized as being the most important pieces of literature. Postcolonial critics revisit canons constructed by Europeans to see where and when native literature has been omitted or underrepresented. They write anthologies of minoritized writers' works to highlight their importance. And they re-evaluate the ideas of the critics who wrote negatively about literature and the arts of racialized populations.

A postcolonial critic should pay attention to the fact that the reader's social, ethnic, and cultural background determines his or her interpretation of a text in the process of reading. Readers, consequently, are actively involved in the process of formation of a literature, a literary taste, and a standard of interpretation. The fact is today's dominant canons and criteria for aesthetic judgment have been created through a European lens, which often falls short of comprehending and appreciating non-European art and literature. It is thus important to ask if the readers of a work are white or of color, what literary expectations do they have when engaging with the text, what cultural assumptions those expectations are based on, and how the positionality of the readers contributes to the process of judging the quality or the significance of the work:

4-1- What are major European interpretations of minority, indigenous, colonial, or postcolonial literary (or artistic) works? How much of those readings were subjective (and perhaps inaccurate) because of the cultural background of European critics, commentators, or historians? Did those interpretations change over time? Are there any alternative views of the same literature (perhaps offered by local readers and cultural insiders)?

Postcolonial critics, accordingly, explore the process of reading as a collective activity guided (or misguided) by subjective and biased definitions of "great literature". They, in other words, examine the fabrication of "the canon" and also how, in the process, literatures of the minoritized are excluded from mainstream. In the following passage, Nigerian critic Chinua Achebe describes the status of the invisibility of non-European literatures even among the academic elite:

> In the fall of 1974 I was walking one day from the English Department at the University of Massachusetts to a parking lot. It was a fine autumn morning such as encouraged friendliness to passing strangers. Brisk youngsters were hurrying in all directions, many of them obviously freshmen in their first flush on enthusiasm. An older man going the same way as I turned and remarked to me how very young they came these days. I agreed. Then he asked me if I was a student too. I said no I was a teacher. What did I teach? African literature. Now that was funny, he said, because he knew a fellow who taught the same thing, or perhaps it was African history, in a certain community college not far from here. It always surprised him, he went on to say, because he never had thought of Africa as having that kind of stuff. (From *Hopes and Impediments: Selected Essays* (1965-1987))

It is important that emerging postcolonial critics revive the significance of indigenous art and literature by recollecting and reframing them. For instance, after the withdrawal of colonial cultural control, postcolonial intellectuals have attempted to put together scattered and hidden pieces of indigenous literature in solid textual bodies such as **anthologies** in order to increase visibility and access for readers.

Artistic Indigenous products have usually been degraded by European notions of "fine art" and native artists have usually been regarded as lower rate. Emerging postcolonial critics should engage with reassessments of popular art, folk art, and native cultural products to undermine colonial aesthetic notions. Such an engagement would help rediscover and recognize artistic and literary forms that are not necessarily practiced in European art forms. Creating anthologies can revive indigenous literary forms and practices that have been underrepresented. Collection creation can also support native artistic movements or literary waves. One famous example of such an attempt from African American literature is Alain Locke's *The New Negro: An Interpretation*, published in 1925. The book is a collection of African American art, music, and literature, which significantly contributed to the Harlem Renaissance. Today, fortunately, there are many more anthologies that similarly present different postcolonial literatures. Creation of anthologies is an important enough critical activity to require a question on its own:

4-2- In artistic or literary areas of your interest, are there possibilities for collecting a number of works in a single body to revive and give prominence to underrated non-European literatures? In case of currently dominant anthologies, is there room for reassessment and critique?

An attempt to unearth or create an indigenous literature can lead critics to engage with comparative studies of different literatures impacted by colonialism. It can also have critics compare and contrast indigenous literary trends with those in European literature.

This tendency has attracted many postcolonial thinkers to a field of study known as **comparative literature**.

Emerging postcolonial critics can compare bodies of literature produced by the colonized (or the previously colonized) and the minoritized to see whether there are shared themes or other similarities. Similarities between the literatures of colonized and oppressed populations can help us understand the challenges and dynamics of colonization on a global scale. The contrasts also can teach us about each individual context, the conceptual interests of different intellectual communities, and also the stylistic traditions unique to each culture.

On the other hand, a comparison between mainstream Western literary traditions with those of the colonized, the minoritized, the racialized, or the marginalized, can show the extent of the presence of the culture of the **metropolis**, the mother country, in aboriginal or minority literatures as well as the impact of indigenous cultures on mainstream literary products. It is interesting to see how these bodies of literature challenge one another or merge and coexist in aesthetic harmony.

To highlight the importance of comparative studies of literature in postcolonial literary criticism, let us end our section about readership and the canon with the following question:

4-3 What can a comparative study of literatures penned by the colonized or the minoritized tell us about colonialism and/or racism? What can such a study teach us about the unique characteristics of an indigenous or ethnic literary tradition in terms of topic and style? Also what can a comparative study of a native literature with mainstream European literature tell us about aesthetic and conceptual give and take between the two traditions?

5- Historical And Biographical Evidence

Postcolonial criticism is not a literary theory interested in aesthetic craftsmanship only; it advocates a political, social, and cultural investigation into the experiences of colonized and minoritized peoples and individuals. Furthermore, culture, art, and literature are not produced in an aesthetic vacuum but grow in sociocultural contexts that need to be examined for reliable knowledge of cultural products. Literary analysis of a text is only meaningful when a critic examines the text as one piece in a jigsaw puzzle of **social, historical, economic, and political discourses**. Therefore, any piece of **historical evidence** might turn out to be quite useful in understanding the world of a literary work. Such evidence in postcolonial criticism could include representations of native political structures and economic systems, or indigenous beliefs, philosophies, social practices, art, technology, and any other piece of information that is likely to help correct colonizers' presentations of the "other", or the minoritized and the marginalized.

Another important investigation is an attempt to find similarities between the histories of the nations that have experienced colonialism. This can help us formulate the mechanisms of colonialism and work out repeated patterns in phenomena such as discrimination, slavery, or immigration.

Next to historical evidence, biographical information about the authors of the works under examination can strengthen textual analyses and interpretations. It is important to see to which side of the conflict the writer belongs in order to make biases explicit. **Biographical evidence** can help us identify the out-of-text ideologies that the writer has consciously or unconsciously brought into his or her work. If a critic, for instance, reaches the conclusion that *Robinson Crusoe* has a colonialist agenda, their argument would benefit from examining if Daniel Defoe's Puritan background had leaked into the novel, by highlighting the white man's "superiority" thanks to his "superior" faith, as was believed by the Puritans.

It is important to consider whether the writer is white or of color or whether the writer is addressing a white or non-white audience. The question of background might sometimes become more complicated. For instance, in case of canonized indigenous or minoritized writers, a critic could ask if they have gained acclaim by adopting European taste or promulgating European beliefs.

Although the text itself is usually the main inspiration for postcolonial literary analysis, emerging critics should be encouraged to gather historical and economic evidence to underline colonial mechanisms and experiences in the text:

> **5-1 How can studying the historical circumstances of the time when the work was written help us better understand the text and also colonial dynamics? How can the author's personal background help us identify the ideologies presented in the text? How can historical comparisons between peoples who share colonial experiences help us formulate universal dynamics of colonialism and common patterns of occupation, racism, and discrimination.**

6- Positionality

When discussing biographical evidence in the previous section, it was recommended that emerging postcolonial critics should think about who the authors that they read are in order to study their position in colonial relations, or their **positionality**. A focus on positionality in postcolonial criticism is important because readers who are interested in undistorted accounts of colonial dynamics need to read the writers who experienced colonialism first-hand as members of minority groups. History of colonialism has traditionally been written and told by colonizers, who have actively excluded the voices of the colonized and the minoritized. Sensitivity about the positionality of the writer, thus, hails from centuries of being silenced as "the other." Whereas in the previous section, we discussed the positionality of the author, here we highlight the significance of the positionality of the postcolonial critic.

It is important to remember that postcolonial criticism, at least what we recognize as such in English and other European languages, has been basically a Western phenomenon. Many influential publications on postcolonial theory have been written and disseminated by thinkers in Western academia. Western academics and activists have long had a **savior mentality**, which has not led to great results. This **savior complex** has often been criticized by non-white populations residing outside Europe and settler colonial lands such as the United States, Canada, and Australia.

Indigenous intellectuals have frequently expressed their dissatisfaction with the activities of **white saviors**, who appear to believe that they know the problems of the people of color and the way to fix them better than the members of minority communities. The same is also true of people of color living in the West, working in American and European universities, and publishing (and presenting) in European languages for an elite academic audience. Such engagements have also been skeptically described as opening the Western academia up for further cultural imperialism. The critics, for instance, argue that Western postcolonial theory has historically provided a gloomy picture of the process of decolonization. Think, for example, of the concepts introduced in this very handbook. There is in fact very little celebration of independence along the different steps of the process of decolonization, presented as: resistance, mimicry, independence, disillusionment, and double-consciousness.

These considerations make a question about positionality an important aspect of postcolonial theory. Nevertheless, highlighting the concept of positionality is not meant to indicate that the European/white postcolonial critics should not have a share in the conversation. Instead, thinking about this concept might encourage them to be explicit about their positionality. Currently, in many fields of humanities research, novice researchers are instructed to discuss their positionality and their relation to the human populations that their research is about. Postcolonial theory is no exception. Explicit articulation of one's positionality can add to the rigor of a critic's work. Thus, an invitation to reflect on your positionality as an emerging critic is the final question of this pamphlet:

> **6-1- What is the positionality of postcolonial critics/thinkers who might have written about the works you are studying? What are their implicit biases? What are their educational backgrounds and lived experiences? How do you think these biases and experiences have impacted their writing about non-European literary works? Have the critics you are reading, or referencing in your work, been explicit about their positionality, especially if they are white/European critics? Also, what about your positionality as a critic? How does your racial, ethnic, national, or linguistic background relate to the critical piece you are writing or the topic that you are investigating?**

I should not conclude this document without an explicit explanation about my own positionality as the writer of this pamphlet. I would like to state that rather than an expert in postcolonial theory, I am a teacher of literary theory engaging with student populations who have just started to make sense of literary criticism. This pamphlet is the result of me and my students' attempts to make sense of postcolonial theory and to simplify it for classroom activities. Postcolonial topics are very sensitive issues and postcolonial theory has developed in many complex ways and in multiple directions. The pamphlet that you have in your hands does not cover all this complexity and nuance because of its limited scope. It is thus quite understandable if some of the themes of this handbook, or the examples offered to illustrate the topics, seem over-simplified to experts. This handbook has been put together to create interest among emerging critics to engage with more complex publications by familiarizing them with the basic topics discussed in postcolonial theory.

Printed in Great Britain
by Amazon